THE MOST IMPORTANT
DECISION YOU WILL EVER MAKE

THE MOST IMPORTANT DECISION YOU WILL EVER MAKE

*A Complete and Thorough Understanding
of What It Means to Be Born Again*

JOYCE
MEYER

NEW YORK   BOSTON   NASHVILLE

Unless otherwise indicated, all Scripture quotations are taken from the *King James Version* of the Bible.

Scripture quotations marked AMP are taken from *The Amplified Bible, Old Testament* copyright © 1965, 1987 by Zondervan Corporation. *New Testament* copyright © 1958, 1987 by the Lockman Foundation. Used by permission.

Warner Faith

Time Warner Book Group
1271 Avenue of the Americas, New York, NY 10020
Visit our Web site at www.twbookmark.com.

The Warner Faith name and logo are registered trademarks of Warner Books.

Printed in the United States of America

First Warner Faith Printing: February 2003

10 9 8 7 6 5 4 3 2

ISBN: 0-446-69153-4 ISBN 978-0-446-69153-6
LCCN: 2002115547

Contents

~⊙~

1

❧

THE MOST IMPORTANT DECISION YOU WILL EVER MAKE

I would like to talk to you about a very important decision. As a matter of fact, this is the most important decision you will ever be faced with. This decision is more important than where you choose to go to school, your career choice, who you decide to marry, or where you decide to live. This decision concerns eternity. Think about it. Forever is a long, long time.

So many people are only concerned with today or a few months down the road. At best, some are concerned with retirement. I want to go beyond that. I want to talk about "life after death." Are you making any provision for that?

Did you know that you are not just a body made of flesh and bones, blood and muscle? You are a spirit being, you have a soul and you live in a body. When you die, which everyone does sooner or later, your physical body will be put in a grave. It will decay and turn to ashes and dust. But what about "the real you"—the inner you, your personality, your mind, will and emotions?

The spiritual part of you can be thought of as the part of you that cannot be seen with the natural eye. This part of you will live forever. And where the spiritual you lives depends on the decision you make as you read this book.

There are two forces in the world—good and evil, right and wrong. We have a "knowing" of that inside of us even without being told. There are two forces in the spirit realm—God and the Devil; good angels, which are spirit beings created by God to help him carry out His business, and bad angels, called demons.

These bad angels were once good angels who made a choice to rebel against God. Lucifer, an archangel (also called Beelzebub, Satan or the Devil), led these angels in this rebellion, and God threw them out of heaven and created a place for them and their master called hell. (See Rev. 12:7–9.)

God and the good angels have their home in heaven. Satan and the bad angels have their home in hell.

Between heaven and hell is the earth and the atmosphere above the earth. Good and bad angels patrol the earth at all times. Satan also roams about seeking whom he may devour. The Bible tells us that in 1 Peter 5:8. The Holy Spirit of God (God's own Spirit) also dwells on the earth as well as in the heavenlies, and the job God has given Him is to seal, keep, preserve and protect God's people (those who have chosen to serve God). The Holy Spirit also has the job of wooing and winning people who have not yet chosen God and His way of living.

Have you made your choice? The choice is yours. No one can make it for you. God created you with a free will, and He will not force you to choose Him. He did not force the angels. Part of them rebelled, and He let them do what they wanted to do. But remember, *bad choices bring their own penalty.*

2

꧁꧂

ARE YOU BORN AGAIN?

*A*re you born again? What does it mean to be born again? What does the Bible say about being born again? In John 3:3 (AMP) Jesus said,

> "I assure you, most solemnly I tell you, that
> unless a person is born again (anew, from above),
> he cannot ever see (know, be acquainted with,
> and experience) the kingdom of God."

Nicodemus, the man Jesus was speaking to, said, "How can a man be born when he is old? Can he enter his mother's womb again and be born?" (John 3:4 AMP). Perhaps you are thinking the same thing. How can a person be born who has already been born? Jesus is speaking about a spiritual birth. Earlier I said you are a spirit, you have a soul and you live in a body. Your body has already been born, but the Bible teaches that our spirit and soul are dead and dark because of sin.

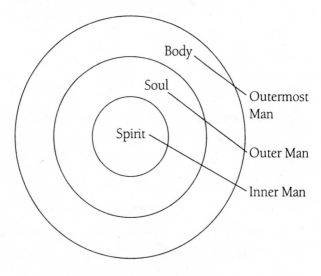

Diagram: Body, Soul and Spirit

You may go look at yourself in the mirror, move your head, arms and legs. You are breathing. You can say you are alive. But is "the real you" alive? Are you alive and full of light *inside*? Do you have peace? Are you at peace with yourself? Do you like yourself? Do you have joy and hope?

Are you afraid to die? These are all questions you need to ask yourself. *You can put a smile on your face and not be smiling inside.*

When Jesus spoke of being born again, He was teaching that the inner man must come alive to God. John 3:6 AMP says, "What is born of [from] the flesh is flesh [of the physical is physical]; and what is born of the Spirit is spirit."

When mothers give birth to babies, they are flesh born of flesh. When God's Holy Spirit comes into your human spirit, you are then spirit born of Spirit. This is referred to as "The New Birth." The Holy Spirit only comes to your spirit *one way*. You can only be born again *one way*. Just as physical birth can only take place one way, so it is with spiritual birth.

You cannot impart spiritual life to yourself anymore than you could cause yourself to be born physically apart from the natural birth process. There is a natural physical process that has to be in operation for a baby to be born, and there is a supernatural (spiritual) process that must be in operation for your spirit to receive new birth.

What is the process? If you decide today that you want to be born again, what do you need to do?

First, recognize and admit that you are spiritually dead due to sin in your life. Romans 3:23 says, "For all have sinned, and come short of the glory of God." *No person is without sin!* Don't be afraid to admit you are a sinner. First John 1:8 AMP says:

> "If we say we have no sin [refusing to admit that we are sinners], we delude *and* lead ourselves astray, and the Truth [which the Gospel presents] is not in us [does not dwell in our hearts]."

Verse 9 AMP says:

> "If we [freely] admit that we have sinned and confess our sins, He is faithful *and* just (true to His own nature and promises) and will forgive our sins [dismiss our lawlessness] and [continuously] cleanse us from all unrighteousness."

Beloved, that is *good* news. No wonder the gospel is referred to as the good news. So we see *Step 1* toward being born again is to *admit* you are a sinner. That means face the truth about yourself. It is hard to face the truth. It hurts to admit our faults. Satan wants to keep you in deception. God wants you to face truth.

Step 2 is *confess* your sins. *Confess* means to speak forth. It has a cleansing effect if you speak forth out of your mouth the things you have done wrong and want to get rid of. Those things are lodged inside of you, and it is those very things, the memory of those things, the sensing of them being wrong, that have filled you with darkness.

Confess them to your Father in heaven. It is God's way of delivering you from them. You get rid of them by confession, and He replaces the sin with forgiveness. He cleanses you. It is like getting a bath inside.

I was born again at age nine, and I vividly remember feeling like I had just been scrubbed on the inside. I felt clean, light, new and fresh inside. Beloved, you can get in the bathtub or shower and give your body a bath. You can scrub your outside clean, but only Jesus can cleanse your inside.

3

Who Is Jesus?

I have mentioned Jesus a few times but have not told you about Him. It is very important that I tell you about Jesus because it is impossible for you to get right with God without knowing Jesus. It is impossible to be born again without knowing Jesus.

I said in the beginning that you have a very important decision to make. Everything about that decision depends on your understanding who Jesus is and knowing what He has done for you. Then your decision is simply whether you want to believe it and receive it or whether you want to continue in darkness the way you are (if you are not born again).

I am getting ready to tell you something that will not make much sense to your head, but your heart will want to believe it. So get ready to hear an amazing true story that can change your life forever.

The Bible says in the Genesis chapters 1 and 2 that in the beginning, God created the first man and called him Adam. God formed his body out of the dust of the ground and breathed into him His own life and Spirit, and Adam became a living soul. In other words, he came alive inside as God breathed into him a portion of His very Self. God's breath was put into the man, and he came alive. He was full of the "Life of God."

God called him "Adam." The Bible says Adam was created in God's image (GEN. 1:26). There were things about Adam that were like God. He had God's breath. He had God's nature and character. He was holy and good like God. No evil was in Adam at all. He and God could fellowship because they were alike.

The Bible says light cannot fellowship with darkness. God and Adam were both light, so they could fellowship together. *Adam was comfortable with God.*

Are you comfortable with God?

Adam was also created with "free choice." God told him what was right but gave him the ability to choose. Adam was good, but to stay good, he had to *continually* choose God and God's ways.

God realized Adam needed a helper, a mate. So He put Adam to sleep and took out one of his ribs, then He closed up his side (GEN. 2:21, 22). From Adam's side, He made woman to be beside (be*side*) Adam as a help, a companion. Notice that woman was not taken out of Adam's feet because he was not to stand on her. She was not taken out of his head to be over him, but she was taken out of his side to be beside him in life as his partner.

Now we have a couple living on earth in a paradise, a beautiful garden God had created just for them. It is pretty obvious that God wanted them to enjoy life.

Are you enjoying life?

There was another creation on the earth, an unpleasant one, Satan, who had previously fallen from God's original plan for him as the archangel of praise and worship. He fell through rebellion and through wanting more than what God had given him. He wanted to be in control, not under God's leadership.

He said he would exalt his throne above God's, and God threw him and the angels who were in rebellion with

13

him out of heaven. Hell was made for them, but Satan plus multitudes of other demon spirits were still given access to earth's atmosphere for a time.

There is a time set aside in God's plan for all of them to be eternally confined in hell, but at this time, God is still allowing the Devil (Satan, Lucifer) access to the earth because men and women are still in the process of *choosing* whom they will serve. In order to have choice, there has to be more than one thing being offered.

God offers life, light, joy, faith, peace, righteousness, hope and all good things. Satan offers death, darkness, despair, depression, devastation, dread, fear and everything bad.

Even as I write these things, I think *why would anyone* choose Satan and his ways? Yet multitudes do. Many people are deceived. They are choosing the wrong way because they lack knowledge. Hosea 4:6 says, "My people are destroyed for lack of knowledge." Perhaps you have not had enough knowledge to make a good choice until now. I am making this truth available with the hope that multiplied thousands will become equipped with the knowledge needed to make a right choice.

Let's go on with our story. Adam and Eve (as Adam named her) were enjoying life in the garden. God gave them charge of the earth. He told them what they could do and could not do; remember, they had free choice. God was telling them what He wanted them to do, telling them how their life could be blessed, but not *forcing* them to do it.

He had placed a lot of fruit-bearing trees in the garden for them to eat freely of, but one tree He told them not to eat the fruit of—"the tree of the knowledge of good and evil" (GEN. 2:17). You might be wondering why God even put the one tree there and told them they should not eat its fruit. Remember, in order to have choice, you must have more than one selection. If they were going to choose to obey God, they had to have something they could choose to disobey.

God wanted their love and obedience. Obedience is actually a fruit of love. He wanted it, but it meant nothing to God if it was not freely given as an act of their free will, as a result of their own choosing.

Would you be excited and blessed if others loved you because you forced them to by leaving them no other choice? God created man with free choice, and He left a few very important choices. You are in the same situation today. You have a free will, free choice, and a very important decision to make.

To go on with our story, Adam and Eve were enjoying life, enjoying God, the garden, the good fruit, each other and all the other things God had made. Genesis 3 tells us that Satan appeared to Eve in the form of a serpent. She was not afraid of the serpent (snake) like you or I might be today. The serpent was not a bad animal. Satan was using it or it appeared to her in that form.

Through the serpent, he began to pose questions to her that made her wonder (reason—the kind of "reasonings" that 2 Cor. 10:4,5 talks about which set themselves up against the true knowledge of God) why God told them not to eat of the tree of the knowledge of good and evil. Actually, God did not want them to ever know anything about evil. But remember, they had to have a choice.

God had told Adam that if he ate of the tree of the knowledge of good and evil *he would surely die.* (GEN. 2:17.) He meant that they would die inside, not their physical body. He meant the life in them would die out. The light would go out, and they would be dark.

Recently a man who had lived a terribly sinful life was being operated on. He thought he might die, and he wanted to get right with God. As Dave and I talked to him, he said, "I feel dead inside."

Think about it. He wanted to be born again because he was afraid he was going to die (physical death) on the operating table, yet in reality, he had been dead all of his life inside, and he said so with his own mouth.

Are you alive or dead?

The serpent lied to Eve. He said, "You shall not surely die" (GEN. 3:4 AMP). What he said was the *opposite* of what God said; therefore, it was a lie. God's Word is truth. And here in the beginning, you can see the nature of Satan. He is the exact opposite of everything God is. God wants you to have everything good. Satan wants to destroy you. He accomplishes this through lies and deception today, the same as he did with Eve.

He continued to deceive and lie and pose questions to her that caused her to get into reasoning ("reasonings" which set themselves up against the true knowledge of God). Eventually she followed the Devil's advice and talked her husband into doing the same. They both disobeyed

God by eating of the fruit He told them to stay away from. The result was exactly what God said—they died spiritually.

The next time God came into the garden to visit Adam and Eve, they hid from Him because they were afraid.

Have you been hiding from God because you are afraid?

As soon as God realized they were afraid, He knew they had sinned. They had believed Satan's lies. They had fallen into the temptation and were now having the fruit of their choice. Fear is the fruit or result of sin.

You may have the fruit of your choice.
But remember, some of it may be bitter in your mouth!

God began to deal with them concerning their sin, but He also had an immediate plan for their redemption and deliverance from this mess they had gotten themselves into. In Genesis 3:15, God told the serpent that the offspring (seed of woman) would bruise his head, and he (Satan) would bruise the heel of the offspring.

He was speaking of Jesus, His only begotten Son, who was already in existence spiritually. God is a Triune God. We refer to Him as "The Trinity": one God in three persons—

Father, Son and Holy Spirit. Each one of the Holy Persons of the Godhead has a major role in your life.

Jesus already existed spiritually, but in order to help man out of the mess he was in, Jesus would eventually need to come to earth. He would need to get inside a natural human body like yours and mine. He would need to humble and lower Himself to become a human being. Remember, Jesus is all God, the Son of God. In other words, *very God of very God*. He certainly was and is very much God.

A plan was birthed, but it would not occur until the exact, right timing in God's overall plan. Ephesians 3:10 (as based on the wording in *The Amplified Bible*) reveals the purpose of God, which is that through the Church,[1] God's wisdom (His many faceted and infinite variety of wisdom) and greatness might be made known to the principalities and powers which are the demon spirits and their ruler, Satan, who rebelled.

In plain English, we are *in a war—a war between Satan and God!* It is already established, and always has been, who wins the war. God does. The victory party is planned.

1. The Church is not a building. It is made up of all born-again believers who ever lived.

Whose side are you fighting on?

If you are serving Satan and are believing his lies, you are working for a loser. God has the winning team.

Anyway, this is ultimately God's plan. He will use born-again people—people who love, obey and serve Him *willingly*—to defeat and completely overthrow Satan and his demon hosts.

You may wonder why God dragged us into this war. Remember, Satan defeated God's man in the garden and stole from him what God wanted him to have. Actually man, through deception, gave it to the Devil. It would be illegal for God to take it away from the Devil and give it back to man.

What God is doing and has been doing since the garden and will keep doing until the job is done is this: *He is equipping man with the ability to regain what Satan stole from him.*

Jesus is the key to the whole plan.

Let me continue our story from Genesis 3 when God told the serpent that eventually his head would be crushed. (That means his authority destroyed.) God had spoken forth what would happen, and if God says it, eventually it happens.

But before it happened, 2,000 years went by while men and women multiplied on the earth. Sin multiplied and trouble multiplied. Where sin multiplies, trouble always multiplies.

Man was unholy now, unrighteous, and no longer right with God. The sin principle dwelt in man's flesh. He had a sin nature. In other words, that was the natural thing for man to do. Sin was natural for him. He did not have to try to sin; he just would. In fact, he could not stop himself.

Every time children were born, they had the nature of sin in their flesh.[2] Children are not accountable for sin until they reach an age of accountability, which is not at a certain number of years. This refers to whenever they reach an awareness that their actions are actually sin against God, and they have an opportunity to choose God or turn Him down.

I have a sin nature; you have one; every person has one. We get it at birth. We become accountable to God as we become aware of our sin.

2. Man's flesh equals his body and soul.

The Law

God loves His people very much, and He instituted a temporary plan that would suffice for those who loved Him and were choosing Him and His ways—a plan that would enable Him to fellowship with His people again. You see, when sin came in and man died spiritually, man could no longer have proper fellowship with God. God is a spirit being, and we must fellowship with Him in our spirit.

God is light. Man was now full of darkness, so the fellowship, oneness, unity and the relationship between God and man was broken. The Bible says there was now a breach between God and man—a break in their compatibility. You might say a wall came down between them—a wall of sin.

God devised the law, a system of written rules and regulations that man had to live by if he wanted to be holy enough, right enough to be God's friend. The law was perfect and holy, just and good. It stated clearly what man had to do in order to be holy.

Before Adam sinned, he instinctively knew what God wanted and did not want. They were one in Spirit, one in heart, one in purpose. After man sinned, he was no longer sensitive to God. He was hardened by sin and the results of sin. He no longer knew God's heart. It had to be written down. Man could not do God's will any longer from his heart or out of his spirit. He had to try to please God in his natural ability. But man was unable to keep *all* of the law perfectly because man was no longer perfect and never would be again as long as he lived on the earth.

God's law said, If you break the law in one point, you are guilty of it all (James 2:10). The law was perfect, and to keep it all, man would need to be perfect.

Sacrifices

Since they had the law but could never keep it no matter how hard they tried, God instituted a system of sacrifices they could make to cover and atone (make up) for their mistakes and failures. They were blood sacrifices. The shedding of blood had to be involved. This may sound rather gross, but the reason behind it makes it understandable. When God breathed into Adam the breath of life, he became a living soul, and his blood was filled with life. His blood began to flow through his body. The Bible says, "the life of the flesh is in the blood" (LEV. 17:11). You know this is true. No one lives without blood. If you stop the blood flow, you stop the life.

When Satan tempted Adam and Eve and they chose sin, sin eventually brought death (ROM. 5:12) and all that death represents—sickness, disease, poverty, war, anger, greed and jealousy. *The only thing strong enough to cover death is life.*

When man broke the law and sinned, it was a type of death. The only atonement for sin was blood sacrifice because the life is in the blood (LEV. 17:11).

Another reason why God did this was a certain type of "looking forward" to the good plan He had in mind for them that would be fulfilled in His perfect timing. The prophets were prophesying about the coming of a Messiah, a Savior, a Redeemer, One Who would deliver them. God was getting the message out. Remember, if God says it, He eventually does it.

This Messiah would become their sacrifice, the final sacrifice, a perfect sacrifice. He would be the sacrificial, perfect, flawless lamb of God. No longer would they need to offer lambs without blemish on the altars in the temple as a sacrifice for their sin. Jesus would come and be the last sacrifice, the final sacrifice. His sacrifice would put an end to the system of the law.

Let me quote you just one of those prophecies.

Isaiah 53:3–7 AMP

"He was despised and rejected and forsaken by men, a Man of sorrows and pains, and acquainted with grief and sickness; and like One from Whom men hide their faces He was despised, and we did not appreciate His worth or have any esteem for Him.

"Surely He has borne our griefs (sicknesses, weaknesses and distresses) and carried our sorrows and pains [of punishment], yet we [ignorantly] considered Him stricken, smitten, and afflicted by God [as if with leprosy].

"But He was wounded for our transgressions, He was bruised for our guilt and iniquities; the chastisement [needful to obtain] peace and well-being for us was upon Him, and with the stripes [that wounded] Him we are healed and made whole.

"All we like sheep have gone astray, we have
turned every one to his own way; and the Lord
has made to light upon Him the guilt and
iniquity of us all.

"He was oppressed, [yet when] He was afflicted,
He was submissive and opened not His mouth;
like a lamb that is led to the slaughter, and as a
sheep before her shearers is dumb, so He opened
not His mouth."

The prophecies were being given. People were waiting
for their Messiah, their Savior, and Deliverer. I do not believe
they even truly understood what they were waiting for.

They did not understand He would deliver them from
the law, from the "works" involved in trying to please God
with perfection when it is impossible to do. They did not
understand that He, Jesus, the Messiah, Savior of the
world, would shed His own blood on a cross, let His blood
flow, *pouring out His life to remove all sin* from every generation.[3] They were waiting, but did not really know what
they were waiting for.

3. Remember that the life is in the blood (LEV. 17:11).

Jesus Comes

God's time came. The Holy Spirit appeared to a young virgin named Mary. She became pregnant by the miracle-working power of God—pregnant with Jesus, the Son of God. It had to happen this way.

Jesus was already in heaven spiritually and had always been. He was with God from the beginning. But now He was going to take on flesh so He could help the rest of the fleshly humans who were in a mess that they had no way out of without a Savior.

John 1:1,14 says that Jesus is the Word of God and that the Word of God became flesh and dwelt among men. Hebrews 4:15 says Jesus is a High Priest who understands our weaknesses and failures because He, having had a fleshly body and a natural soul, was tempted in all points just like we are, *yet without sin*. Beloved, this is the big difference.

Jesus was alive to God inside, totally connected with the Father. He was one with Him, like Adam was before he sinned. The Bible calls Him the second Adam. (See 1 Corinthians 15:45,47.) Romans 5:12–21 says if one man's (Adam) sin caused all men to sin, then how much more can one man's (Jesus) righteousness make all men right with God?

27

Adam's sin came down on you from generation to generation. Now, *if you will believe it,* the second Adam, Jesus, is waiting to give you His righteousness. Adam was a man, full of God, full of God's life. Sin came and man was filled with darkness. The light in him went out.

Are you full of darkness or light?

Jesus was also a man, born of a woman, but He was full of God. Adam sinned. Jesus did not ever sin; He was a perfect sacrifice for sin.

The Old Testament believers had to constantly make sacrifices for their sin, but the guilt was always there.

Do you feel guilty or free? Dirty or clean?

Jesus became the sinless lamb, the sacrificial lamb of God that took away the sin of the world. Hebrews 10:11–14 AMP says:

> "Furthermore, every [human] priest stands [at his altar of service] ministering daily, offering the same sacrifices over and over again, which never are able to strip [from every side of us] the sins [that envelop us] and take them away—

28

"Whereas this One [Christ], after He had offered a single sacrifice for our sins [that shall avail] for all time, sat down at the right hand of God,

"Then to wait until His enemies should be made a stool beneath His feet.

"For by a single offering He has forever completely cleansed and perfected those who are consecrated and made holy."

The Old Testament priests offered the sacrifices on behalf of the people. They had to do it over and over, all the time, always working, trying to be good, always failing, never feeling good about themselves (inwardly), always trying to *be* good so they could *feel* good.

But Hebrews shows us that Jesus offered Himself once and for all, a perfect sacrifice. He kept all the law. *His victory is available to all who will believe.*

4

❧

WHAT SHOULD
YOU BELIEVE?

*B*elieve that Jesus did what the Bible says. Believe He is indeed the Son of God, born of a virgin. He took man's sin on Himself. He became our sacrifice and died on the cross. He did not stay dead. He was in the grave three days. During that time, He entered hell and defeated Satan.

All this He did willingly because He loved His Father (God) and because God and Jesus loved you and me so much that no plan was too extreme. Whatever it took to get God's people back, free again, is what They would do. *Jesus paid* for our sins on the cross and went to hell in our place. Then, as God had promised, on the third day Jesus rose from the dead.

What Happened on the Cross

When Jesus hung on the cross, He took our sin upon Himself. God cannot stay in the presence of sin. As Jesus took our sin, He was separated from the presence of the Father. The same thing happened to Adam in the garden. As he sinned, the presence of God left him. God cannot dwell in the midst of sin. Sin puts a wall between man and God.

Jesus was taking your sins and those of everyone else upon Him as He felt this absence of His Father's presence. He said, "My God, my God, why have you forsaken me?" (See MATT. 27:46, author's paraphrase). Jesus knew it would happen, but the horror of separation from the bright presence of the Father was worse than He could have imagined, and it caused Him to cry out. He committed His Spirit to the Father and died. So they put Him—that is, His body—in a grave, and His spirit went to hell because that is where we deserved to go.

Remember in the very beginning of this book, I said that when you die, only your body dies. The rest of you, your soul and spirit, goes either to heaven or hell.

There is no hope of anyone going to heaven unless they believe this truth. You cannot go to heaven unless you believe with all your heart that Jesus took your place. *He became your substitute and took all the punishment you deserve. He bore all your sins. He paid the debt you owe.*

He did it for you because He loves you. John 3:16 says:

> "For God so loved the world, that he gave his only begotten Son, that whosoever believeth in him should not perish, but have everlasting life."

Jesus went to hell for *you*. He died for *you*. He paid for *your* sins. God was faithful to Jesus. God did what He told Jesus He would do. He raised Him from the dead.

But until that happened, He was alone for three days satisfying the courts of justice and conquering the hosts of hell. He took the keys of hell and death. He preached to the prisoners held captive there about paradise. He led them out victorious.

On the third day, He rose from the dead. After that, He entered into the heavenlies with some of His own blood and placed it there as a constant reminder that sin-less blood had been shed to pay for man's sin because the life is in the blood (LEV. 17:11).

Back To Believing

What else do you need to believe?

Believe He did it for you.

Believe it with your heart. Your head will not grasp what I am telling you, but believe it with your heart. Listen to your heart (your spirit).

Romans 10:9 says that if you confess with your mouth that Jesus is Lord and believe with your heart that God raised Him from the dead, you will be saved (born again).

At this point, if you have decided that you believe what I am telling you and you want to receive Jesus, you need to say: *I believe Jesus is the Son of God. I believe He died for me. I believe God raised Him from the dead.*

Romans 10:10 (AMP) says that with the heart man believes and is justified. The word *justified* means made as if he never sinned; it means cleansed, made right with God. Only believing in Jesus and all He did will justify you.

No amount of good works will ever make you right with God. Merely going to church will not justify you. First, you must be justified through faith, then the good works will follow as a sign of your heart change. The heart must be right first. You *must* believe with your heart, your inner man.

Romans 10:10 (AMP) further says to confess with your mouth to confirm your salvation. *Confirm* means "establish."[1] Saying what you believe secures it as yours. It sort of nails it down, so to speak.

Summary

To be born again you must believe:

- God is. (GEN. 1:1; HEB. 11:6.)

- Jesus is the Son of God, born of a virgin, born of flesh and blood. (MATT. 1:18; MATT. 1:23.)

- Jesus is God, one part of the Trinity, one part of the Triune Godhead. (COL. 2:9,10; HEB. 1:5–8.)

1. W. E. Vine, *An Expository Dictionary of New Testament Words* (Old Tappan, New Jersey: Fleming H. Revell Company, 1940), p. 226.

- He came in a fleshly body so He could help man. (JOHN 1:1; JOHN 1:14; LUKE 4:18–21.)

- He took on Himself all your sins, bore them in His own body on the cross. (ISA. 53:4,5; 2 COR. 5:21.)

- He died for your sins. (HEB. 2:9.)

- He went to hell in your place and gained victory there, triumphing over the enemy. (ACTS 2:31.)

- On the third day, He arose again from the dead. (LUKE 24:1–7; ACTS 2:32.)

- He is now seated at the right hand of the Father in heaven. (HEB. 10:12.)

- He is available to every person who will believe. (ROM. 10:13; JOHN 1:12.)

- He will come to live in you by the power and presence of the Holy Spirit living in your human spirit, once again making you alive to God. (ROM. 8:14–16.)[2]

---

2. Note: You are encouraged to look up these Scriptures if you have a Bible. Let the Word of God convince you.

This is what it means to be born again.

If you believe this, then you can:

- Proceed by admitting you are a sinner in need of a Savior. (ROM. 3:23,24.)

- Now confess your sins to God. (1 JOHN 1:9.)

- Have a repentant attitude—a willingness to turn from your sin and be willing to live a new life for God. (ACTS 3:19.)

Let's Pray

James 4:2 says you have not because you ask not. *Ask Jesus into your heart; ask Him to forgive your sins.* He will forgive you, and He will come to live in your spirit. Your spirit will come alive to God. Here is a sample prayer you may pray. However, I encourage you to pour your heart out to God in your own way.

Father God, I believe Jesus Christ is Your Son, the Savior of the world. I believe He died on the cross for me, and He bore all of my sins. He went to

hell and triumphed over death and the grave.
I believe Jesus was resurrected from the dead
and is now seated at Your right hand. I need You,
Jesus. Forgive my sins, save me, come to live
inside of me. I want to be born again.

If you believe these truths and have followed the
guidelines:

Congratulations,
you are born again!

5

✺

Now That I Am Born Again, What Should I Do?

Grow

*N*ow that you are born again, you need to *grow* as a Christian. You have experienced "The New Birth," so you are a baby Christian. God's desire for you is that you grow up and be mature—a full grown believer that walks in God's ways, knows the Word of God and knows how to hear the voice of God.

Learn the Word

This cannot happen unless you have the Word. Your spirit and soul (the inner you) needs to be fed and nourished so it will get strong. It also needs exercise. The same as your body needs food and exercise to stay strong and healthy, your spirit and soul also need food and exercise.

Exercise

The Word of God (the Bible) is the spiritual food you need. Spiritual exercise consists of things like praying, singing praise to God, confessing the Word, thinking about the goodness of God, thinking about the Word, giving and fellowshipping with other Christians.

Pray

Ask God to lead you to a good church where you can begin to learn His Word. Start to read the Bible. There are many modern translations available today that make the Bible more easily understood than in the past. I like *The*

Amplified Bible; however, there are many other translations available. Go to a Christian bookstore and select one. As you begin to read the Bible, ask the Holy Spirit (God's Spirit) to help you understand it.

As you begin your new life with God, talk to Him. He is *always* with you. You will never be alone again. Jesus said, "I will never leave thee, nor forsake thee" (HEB. 5:13). You do not have to struggle with things like you have in the past. Ask the Lord to help you with everything you do. He is your new Partner in life. The *Holy Spirit* is called the "Helper" in the Bible (JOHN 14:16 AMP).

You may notice I am referring to the Father (God), the Son (Jesus), and the Holy Spirit. To make sure I am not confusing you, let me remind you that you now serve *One God,* a Triune God, a Trinity, and each person of the Godhead has a "special function" in your everyday life.

Pray to the Father in Jesus' Name through the power and leading of the Holy Spirit, Who is now living inside you bringing you the presence and reality of the Father and Son.

Water Baptism

You will need to be baptized as soon as possible. Do not put it off any longer than necessary. The Bible teaches that a person should be baptized after he or she accepts Jesus as Lord and savior.

Baptism means "to submerge in water" and is generally done by a spiritual leader assisting you and praying over you as you go down into the water and are brought back up.

This signifies the burial of the old way of living and is an outward sign of you declaring your decision to live for God. Romans 6 teaches us that we are buried with Christ in the waters of baptism and raised to a new life when we are raised out of the water.

Actually, water baptism is your declaration to the Devil and demon spirits (remember, they roam the earth and fill the earth's atmosphere even though you cannot see them) that you have made a decision to follow Jesus. He is now your Lord. You are burying your old, sinful ways and are making a commitment to learn new ways of living. The Bible says that through Jesus' death and resurrection, He opened up a new and living way.

You must be *committed* to these new principles, or the Devil will cause you to backslide. First Peter 3:21 says baptism is a figure of deliverance. That means it cuts you off from the enemy, Satan. It also says you are demonstrating what you believe to be yours in Jesus Christ.

If you are familiar with Moses and the Israelites and their encounter with the Red Sea, God caused them to go down into the sea and come out. They parted the water by a miracle of God. This actually delivered them from the enemy. But as their enemy (Pharaoh and his army) chased them, the enemy was drowned in the Red Sea. This is a type of what happens to you, spiritually speaking, in water baptism.

If you were baptized as a baby, which many people are as a religious formality, I suggest you go ahead and be baptized now that you understand it and can exercise your faith to believe what the Bible says about baptism.

Religious formality means nothing if there is no real faith involved. Religion is the Devil's invention to keep people out of relationship with the Father, Son and Holy Spirit.

Religion is man's idea of God's expectations—a formal system of man-made doctrines (some according to God's

Word and usually some not) that give rules and regulations to follow in order to please God. This system does not impart life to the inner man, and it causes people to get into "works of the flesh" trying to please God.

People begin to follow church rules—things that are good in themselves, but if they have no meaning to the participants, they are lifeless. But now that you have relationship with God through Jesus, you can be baptized, and it will mean something to you because faith is present.

Declare to all that you are burying the old man (your old nature) and all his old ways in baptism.

Special note: You do not have to have an emotional experience with God to be born again. You may or may not experience some kind of specific feelings. Many people express a feeling of cleansing or relief—a feeling that their burdens have been lifted. However, I encourage you to remember that the Bible nowhere tells us to base our faith on feelings. Nor do you need to remember a certain time when you received Jesus. But you *must* know in *your* heart that you *are* born again.

All four of my children are born again, and two of them could not tell you "a time" when they first believed.

They have grown up always knowing Jesus. I certainly believe this is God's best plan. But, thank God, He also has a special plan for those of us who did not have parents who raised us in the nurture and admonition of the Lord.

6

∽

Is There Anything Else?

Yes! There is one more very important thing you need to know.

There is yet another blessing available to you. The Bible calls it the baptism of the Holy Spirit. The Bible tells us that John said when Jesus came, Jesus would baptize people with the Holy Ghost and fire (MATT. 3:4–6, 11). John had been baptizing people in water, and they had been repenting of their sins, but this baptism in the Holy Spirit—what is that?

In Acts 1:5–8 AMP, Jesus talked about this Spirit baptism. He said they would receive power (ability, efficiency, and might) when the Holy Spirit came upon them, and this power would cause them to be witnesses to Jesus.

When you received Jesus, you received the Holy Spirit into your human spirit. But the baptism of the Spirit is a filling completely. He fills you, and you are placed into Him. It is like asking the Spirit to fill you through and through with the power and ability to live the Christian life and serve God according to His will.

The Greek word *dunamis,* translated *power* in Acts, actually means miraculous power, ability, might and strength.[1] Miracle-working power!

Ask yourself: Do I need power, ability, strength and miracles in my life? If you answered "yes," then you need to be baptized in the Holy Spirit.

Special Note: If you have ever been involved in the occult in any way, I ask now that you repent of that activity before pursuing the baptism of the Holy Spirit. Witchcraft, Ouija board, fortune-telling, seances, black or white magic, Eastern religions, cults, astrology, New Age, hypnotism, and psychic visits are practices that the Bible teaches are an abomination to God (DEUT. 18:9–12).

---

1. James Strong, *The Exhaustive Concordance of the Bible* (McLean, Virginia: MacDonald Publishing, 1978), "Greek Dictionary of the New Testament," p. 24, #1411.

Ask God to forgive you of such activity and to cleanse you. Make a declaration with your mouth that you no longer want anything to do with such spirits.

Scriptural References for Being Baptized in the Holy Spirit

ACTS 1:8 AMP

"But you shall receive power (ability, efficiency, and might) when the Holy Spirit has come upon you, and you shall be My witnesses in Jerusalem and all Judea and Samaria and to the ends (the very bounds) of the earth."

ACTS 2:1–4 AMP

"And when the day of Pentecost had fully come, they were all assembled together in one place,

"When suddenly there came a sound from heaven like the rushing of a violent tempest blast, and it filled the whole house in which they were sitting.

"And there appeared to them tongues resembling fire, which were separated and distributed and which settled on each one of them.

"And they were all filled (diffused throughout their souls) with the Holy Spirit and began to speak in other (different, foreign) languages (tongues), as the Spirit kept giving them clear and loud expression [in each tongue in appropriate words]."

ACTS 8:17 AMP

"Then [the apostles] laid their hands on them one by one, and they received the Holy Spirit."

ACTS 10:44–46 AMP

"While Peter was still speaking these words, the Holy Spirit fell on all who were listening to the message.

"And the believers from among the circumcised [the Jews] who came with Peter were surprised and amazed, because the free gift of the Holy

Spirit had been bestowed and poured out largely even on the Gentiles.

"For they heard them talking in [unknown] tongues (languages) and extolling and magnifying God."

ACTS 19:6 AMP

"And as Paul laid his hands upon them, the Holy Spirit came on them; and they spoke in [foreign, unknown] tongues (languages) and prophesied."

Tongues

You probably noticed that people began to speak in "tongues" or "other tongues" as they were baptized in the Holy Spirit.

This means a language other than their usual one. It could be a known tongue (to someone else, not the speaker) or a tongue of angels (one unknown to any human) (1 COR. 13:1). The best and easiest way to describe tongues is to say it is a spiritual language, one the Holy

Spirit knows and chooses to speak through you but one you do not know. It is the Holy Spirit speaking directly to God through you.

Tongues is referred to as a *phenomenon*. That means we do not understand it with our minds. It is a spiritual thing.

Paul said in 1 Corinthians 14:14 that if you pray in tongues, your mind is unfruitful. In chapter 14:4, Paul says when you pray in tongues, you edify (build up) yourself.

Praying in tongues assures you that you can pray a perfect prayer when you are in a situation in which you do not know how to pray as you should. Romans 8:26 AMP says,

> "So too the [Holy] Spirit comes to our aid and
> bears us up in our weakness; for we do not know
> what prayer to offer nor how to offer it worthily
> as we ought, but the Spirit Himself goes to meet
> our supplication and pleads in our behalf with
> unspeakable yearnings and groanings too deep
> for utterance."

Praying in tongues strengthens your spirit. It builds you up spiritually. Jude 1:20 (AMP) says:

"But you, beloved, build yourselves up [founded] on your most holy faith [make progress, rise like an edifice higher and higher], praying in the Holy Spirit."

Laying on of Hands

You may receive the Holy Spirit by having someone who believes in the doctrine of the baptism of the Holy Spirit with the evidence of speaking in other tongues lay hands on you and pray for you.

By Faith

Luke 11:13 (AMP) tells us:

"If you then, evil as you are, know how to give good gifts [gifts that are to their advantage] to your children, how much more will your heavenly Father give the Holy Spirit to those who ask and continue to ask Him!"

Therefore, ask. You may ask God yourself.

The Holy Spirit May Come Sovereignly

I received the baptism of the Holy Spirit in my car in February, 1976, as a sovereign move of God in my life. I was crying out to God asking for more of Him. I said, "God, there has to be more to Christianity than I am experiencing." I wanted victory over my problems, and I did not have it.

I was born again many years before receiving the baptism of the Holy Spirit. I was saved and would have gone to heaven had I died. Yet I was without *power* to live a victorious Christian life. I cried out in desperation that morning, and that same evening, Jesus baptized me in the Holy Spirit.

I did not speak in tongues right away (mainly because I knew *nothing* about such things). It probably would have frightened me at that time. However, I did receive much power, ability, determination and understanding. During the next three weeks, God led me to radio programs and books where I learned about this baptism in the Spirit.

At first, I did not know what had happened to me. I just knew it was wonderful, and it was of God. I then learned about speaking in tongues, asked God for it and received.

How to Receive Tongues

Ask God to fill you and to baptize you in the Holy Spirit. Simply pray, *Father, in Jesus' Name, I ask you to baptize me in the power of the Holy Spirit with the evidence of speaking in tongues.*

Be relaxed and at ease in God's presence. He loves you and wants you to have His best. Wait on Him quietly and believe you are receiving. Believe before you *feel* any change. You may *feel* a change taking place, but you may not. Do not be led by your feelings; be led by God's promises.

To speak in tongues, open your mouth, and as the Spirit gives you utterance, speak forth what you hear coming up out of your inner man. *This will not come out of your head.* Remember, your mind does not understand this.

That is why it is so hard for many people. We are accustomed to our minds running our lives. This whole book is about spiritual life and learning to live spiritually, not naturally.

You will hear or sense syllables, phrases, groanings or utterances that are unusual sounding or foreign sounding to you. Take a step of faith and utter them; speak them forth. Acts 2:4 says, "*they* . . . began to speak with other tongues, as the Spirit gave them utterance."

You may now use this language (which will grow as you grow and as you exercise the gift) anytime you pray or just to edify yourself. Do not speak in tongues around people who do not understand. Tongues brought forth in a church setting should be interpreted or explained.

Enjoy your new life in the Spirit!

Note:
If you have any questions, feel free to
contact my office.

Did You Make the Right Decision?

If you received Jesus or the baptism of the Holy Spirit as a
result of reading this book, please call or write and let us
know. It will encourage us. We would like to pray for you
and rejoice with you.

*Smile, Jesus
Loves
You!*

". . . choose for yourselves this day whom you will serve . . . but as for me and my house, we will serve the Lord."

JOSHUA 24:15 AMP

As you begin your new walk with God, it is important that you receive sound, spiritual teaching on a regular basis. The Word of God is the spiritual food you need for spiritual growth.

Beloved, John 8:31,32 AMP says, "If you abide in My word . . . you are truly My disciples. And you will know the Truth, and the Truth will set you free."

I exhort you to take hold of God's Word, plant it deep in your heart, and according to 2 Corinthians 3:18, as you look into the Word, you will be transformed into the image of Jesus Christ.

With Love,

Joyce

About the Author

JOYCE MEYER has been teaching the Word of God since 1976 and in full-time ministry since 1980. She is the bestselling author of more than fifty inspirational books, including *How to Hear from God*, *Knowing God Intimately*, and *Battlefield of the Mind*. She has also released thousands of teaching cassettes and a complete video library. Joyce's *Enjoying Everyday Life* radio and television programs are broadcast around the world, and she travels extensively conducting conferences. Joyce and her husband, Dave, are the parents of four grown children and make their home in St. Louis, Missouri.

To contact the author write:

Joyce Meyer Ministries
P. O. Box 655
Fenton, Missouri 63026
or call: (636) 349-0303
Internet Address: www.joycemeyer.org

Your prayer requests are welcome.

To contact the author
in Canada, please write:
Joyce Meyer Ministries Canada, Inc.
Lambeth Box 1300
London, ON N6P 1T5
or call: (636) 349-0303

In Australia, please write:
Joyce Meyer Ministries—Australia
Locked Bag 77
Mansfield Delivery Centre
Queensland 4122
or call: 07 3349 1200

In England, please write:
Joyce Meyer Ministries
P. O. Box 1549
Windsor
SL4 1GT
or call: (0) 1753-831102

JOYCE MEYER TITLES

Printed in the United States
141339LV00001B/109/P

9 780446 691536